BRITISH MILITARY BAN

The
HOUSEH OLD
DIVISION

WENDY SKILTON

Midland Publishing

CONTENTS

THE AUTHOR

Wendy Skilton is a Director of Music in Miniature, a military figurine company specialising in bands of the British armed forces.

She is a confirmed Royalist with a deep passion for preserving military traditions, customs and legacies and the National Heritage of Britain. She is a member of the International Military Music Society and has had several articles published on British Military Bands

Wendy is married with two daughters and lives with her husband in Leicestershire.

ACKNOWLEDGEMENTS

My thanks are due to all the Directors of Music and the many Bandsmen who have helped in compiling the information for this book, in particular my sincere thanks to Major Roger Tomlinson (Blues & Royals) whose help has been invaluable.

My sincere thanks must also go to Alan Caton, whose patience and help in providing information for this book is very much appreciated.

Finally, I would like to express my sincere gratitude to Frank Tyler who has generously allowed some of his excellent photographs to be reproduced. All other photographs are from my collection.

Wendy Skilton 1992

Illustration captions:

Front cover: *Drum Major in State Dress, Coldstream Guards*

Title page: *'Cladius', a past Drum Horse of the Blues & Royals, on parade at Knightsbridge Barracks.* ALAN CATON

Back cover: *'Caractacus', a Drum Horse of the Blues & Royals, in Review Order, taken at the Royal Tournament 1991*

First published in the UK in 1992 by
Midland Publishing Limited
24 The Hollow, Earl Shilton, Leicester, LE9 7NA

ISBN 1 85780 007 9

© Wendy Skilton 1992

Design by Words & Images, Speldhurst, Kent, and Midland Publishing Limited.
Printed and bound in England by
Printhaus Book Company, Northampton.

INTRODUCTION

Trumpet Major, Life Guards, in Full Dismounted Review Order. Note the badges of rank on the lower right sleeve, which are unusual. Frank Tyler

The Household Cavalry and the Brigade of Guards are unique to this country and nowhere else in the world can one see a finer display of military precision, pageantry and panache than when these famous regiments are on parade in their ceremonial uniforms. Whether on the battlefield, or the parade ground, the Household Regiments are impressive and are an integral part of our national heritage.

The Regimental Bands have a universal reputation for their musical prowess. In the United Kingdom they provide the marching and mounted bands for all of Her Majesty's ceremonial occasions, such as Trooping the Colour, Beating Retreat and Guard Mounting duties. For State visits and Investitures at Buckingham Palace they provide orchestras and quartets. When not so engaged, they travel the country and abroad providing Dance and Concert Bands for all functions, attend broadcasting sessions for the radio and television, record their music onto records, tapes and compact disc, and in between find the time to practice on their instruments and train for their secondary role as medics!

On active service all musicians are trained as medical orderlies, to assist at the front line of battle. However, there are occasions when they are called upon to help the public, such as during the ambulance drivers' strike of 1979 when they were called upon to fill in for the service. Pipers and drummers of the Corps of Drums and Pipes are different in that they are all trained soldiers who take their place with the remainder of their Regiment in times of conflict.

Musicians are trained under the supervision of their regimental Directors of Music and at the Royal Military School of Music, Kneller Hall. However, most of them begin life as Junior Musicians at the Guards Depot, Pirbright.

The Junior Musicians Wing at the Guards Depot was established in June 1965. It is here that all young musicians between the ages of 16 and 17 years enter the training programme after successfully passing the entrance examination and audition. All types of instruments and music are taught here, with emphasis on orchestral performance. In addition the young musicians undergo a rigorous syllabus that includes instru-

Rear views of Bandsmen from Life Guard, Blues & Royals and Scots Guards, at the Royal Military School of Music, Kneller Hall.

mental instruction, musical theory, aural training, basic military training and numerous general educational subjects. On completion, it is customary for the Junior Musicians to attend a further course at the Royal Military School of Music, Kneller Hall.

The Royal Military School of Music was established in 1857 by Field Marshal HRH the Duke of Cambridge, who was then the Commander in Chief of the British Army. The obvious choice for a permanent residence for the school was Kneller Hall at Twickenham. Originally built by Sir Christopher Wren in 1709 as the country house for Sir Godfrey Kneller, it was tragically burned down and had to be rebuilt during the 1840s.

There are two courses available at Kneller Hall: the Pupils' Course and the Student Bandmasters' Course. The Pupils' Course is primarily for the more promising young military musicians and lasts for one year. The Student Bandmasters' Course is for the more experienced military musicians who have been recommended on their excellent musical ability to become a future Bandmaster of one of the Army's Regimental Bands and it lasts for three years. The Bandmasters' Course is also well attended by musicians from military bands all over the world, thus proving conclusively the very high reputation held by The Royal Military School of Music at Kneller Hall.

On completion of their courses, the musicians are now ready to join their Regiment and perform their ceremonial duties. Those who have elected to join the Household Cavalry have to undergo an equestrian course to enable them to play whilst mounted on horseback.

Perhaps the best known of all the ceremonial duties is Trooping the Colour, otherwise known as The Queen's Birthday Parade. The origin of this ceremony can be traced back to 1755 when it was the custom to parade or 'troop' the Regimental Colour in front of the soldiers so they would recognise and rally round it in battle. It was not until 1805 that the parade was first recognised as part of the celebrations for the Sovereign's birthday and it has continued in that capacity ever since. It is during this spectacular ceremony that the massed bands perform one of the most difficult manoeuvres known to the bandsmen, The Wheel. To the spectator it looks as though the musicians are all facing in every direction, with no two going the same way. To the bandsmen it is a complex movement that turns the massed bands a full 90 degrees, and although they have actually performed the movement many of the bandsmen could not tell you how such a complicated movement was accomplished!

Another well-known ceremony in which the Household Bands participate is Beating Retreat, which has its origins in the sixteenth century. A book that was published in 1598 states,

> 'ye Drumme Major will advertise (by beate of drum) those required for watch.'

Later, in 1727, it was customary that

> 'half an hour before the setting of the sun the drummers and Port-Guards are to go upon

the ramparts and beat a retreat to give notice to those without that the gates are to be shut. The Drummers will not take more than a quarter of an hour to Beat Retreat.'

The modern day ceremony of Beating Retreat is a re-creation of those earlier duties, performed at sunset it signals the end of the working day and the mounting of the New Guard.

Top: *Band of the Coldstream Guards at a rehearsal for Trooping the Colour.* Frank Tyler

Above: *Mounted Bands of the Household Cavalry at a rehearsal for Trooping the Colour. Note the full dress helmets worn with the khaki uniform.* Frank Tyler

The Mounted Band of the Blues & Royals leading the Queen's Life Guard to Horse Guards for the Changing of the Guard. They are pictured here passing the Household Cavalry Memorial. Frank Tyler

Other public ceremonial duties in which the Household Regimental Bands take part are State visits, the Opening of Parliament, the Garter Ceremony at Windsor Castle and the Queen's Life Guard.

The Queen's Life Guard is the Sovereign's official bodyguard and it is the duty of the Guard to mount sentry duty to all passageways to the Sovereign's residence. The origin of the Queen's Life Guard dates from the days of the Stuart kings when they resided at Whitehall Palace and has always been the duty of the Household Cavalry. Today the Queen's Life Guard is performed alternately by the Life Guards and the Blues & Royals. Perhaps the most famous recollection of this ceremonial duty in modern times was on Tuesday 20 July 1982 when the Queen's Life Guard, found by the Blues & Royals Mounted Squadron, were blown up by a terrorist bomb when only a hundred yards from Hyde Park Corner. Four troopers and seven horses were killed, but Trumpeter Sullivan and his horse, Gauntlet, miraculously survived. The public were horrified, but the Household Cavalry bravely continued their duties and the Queen's Life Guard has been mounted every day since this horrific attack.

HM The Queen has no better ambassadors for Her Country than the Regimental Bands of the Household Cavalry and the Brigade of Guards. Wherever they perform there is no one that is not stirred by such familiar tunes as 'The British Grenadiers', 'Scipio', 'Hi'lan Laddie' and 'Men of Harlech'.

THE HOUSEHOLD CAVALRY

The Household Cavalry is composed of the two senior regiments of the British Army:

    The Life Guards

    The Blues & Royals

    (Royal Horse Guards & 1st Dragoons)

Each have their own Regimental Band with its own Director of Music and they are the only cavalry regiments who perform their ceremonial duties usually mounted on horses.

The full dress uniform (otherwise known as Review Order) worn by the Household Cavalry has changed very little since 1856, the scarlet tunics of the Life Guards differentiating them from the dark blue tunics of the Blues & Royals. Members of the bands do not wear the cuirass, the close fitting steel plates being too constrictive for them to play their instruments. In addition to the Review Order of dress Trumpeters and bandsmen of the Household Cavalry wear the 'State Dress', the familiar gold and crimson tunic with the dark blue 'jockey cap'. Due to the complexities of the uniforms, a full description will be given under the relevant regiment.

For many ceremonial and public duties the bands parade on foot, however for all State occasions (such as Trooping the Colour) they perform mounted on horses.

For both Regiments all musicians and the Directors of Music are mounted on black horses. It is not certain when this practice first began, however, a contemporary print of 1837 does show the 1st Troop of the Life Guards mounted on black horses at the Coronation of King Charles II. It is known that the 2nd Troop of the Life Guards were mounted on black horses in 1692, but there is no evidence to suggest that this was common to all Troops at that time. By the end of the Napoleonic Wars the Trumpeters were all mounted on grey horses, a common practice throughout all the cavalry regiments.

Today, all the horses purchased by the Royal Army Veterinary Corps on behalf of the Household Cavalry must stand approximately 16 hands high and should be completely black, although white socks on the legs and a little white marking on the face is acceptable. The mounted bands do not have horses of their own, but use those allocated for service within the Household Cavalry, usually the older and quieter mounts. Trumpeters are peculiar in that they are solely mounted on grey horses, thus maintaining the old tradition.

For the musicians of both regiments the harness and saddlery is made of black leather, with brass ornamentation on the head kit. Saddle covers of the Life Guards and the Blues & Royals Regimental Bands are all made of black sheepskin, (only the troopers of the Life Guards have white sheepskin saddle covers). The grey horses of the Trumpeters of the Life Guards have the addition of a scarlet and black horsehair plume, mounted on the harness beneath the throat.

On ceremonial occasions the Directors of Music have the addition of a shabraque, or saddle cloth. For the Life Guards it is dark blue with the regimental cypher and battle honours richly embroidered in each corner, the rounded edges having a border of scarlet and gold lace. The saddle cover is made of black bearskin. The shabraque of the Blues & Royals is scarlet with the regimental cypher and battle honours richly embroidered in each corner, the front being rounded with the rear being pointed. The edges are trimmed with wide gold lace, which has a dark blue line (or 'light') through the centre. The saddle cover is made of black sheepskin and the Director of Music for the Blues & Royals is further distinguished by the horse wearing a black throat plume.

In keeping with tradition each of the two regiments have their own Drum Horses. These will be dealt with under the relevant regiment.

Above: *Band of the Blues & Royals in Gold State Dress, on foot - a very rare sight.* H L Funnell

Mounted Musicians in Full Review Order. Frank Tyler

THE LIFE GUARDS

BATTLE HONOURS

DETTINGEN	ARRAS 1917, 1918
PENINSULA	HINDENBURG LINE
WATERLOO	
TEL-EL-KEBIR	FRANCE AND FLANDERS 1914-18
EGYPT 1882	
RELIEF OF KIMBERLEY	SOULEUVRE
	BRUSSELS
PAARDEBURG	NEDERRIJN
SOUTH AFRICA 1899-1900	NORTH WEST EUROPE 1944-5
MONS	IRAQ 1941
LE CATEAU	PALMYRA
MARNE 1914	SYRIA 1941
AISNE 1914	EL ALAMEIN
MESSINES 1914	NORTH AFRICA 1942-3
YPRES 1914, 1915, 1917	ITALY 1944
SOMME 1916, 1918	

Colonel-in-Chief
HM The Queen

Motto
'Honi soit qui mal y pense' (Evil be to him who evil thinks)

History
Formed on the 8 July 1922 by the amalgamation of the 1st and 2nd Life Guards.

Home Headquarters
Horse Guards, Whitehall, London SW1A 2YA

Regimental Association
Horse Guards, Whitehall, London SW1A 2YA

Regimental Museum
The Household Cavalry Museum, Combermere Barracks, Windsor, Berks.

Marches

Quick march	Milanollo
	Men of Harlech
Slow march	The Life Guards Slow March
Trot Past	Keel Row

Distinctions

The Life Guards are the senior regiment of the British Army, having been initially formed in 1660 upon the restoration of King Charles II.

The Regiment were the first in the British Army to parade with kettledrums, having brought them over upon their return from Holland in 1660.

On the 4 May 1831 King William IV presented a set of silver kettledrums to the 2nd Life Guards. This was followed by a presentation of a further set of silver kettledrums to the 1st Life Guards on 23 July 1831. It is these silver drums that are used on all ceremonial occasions today.

There are a total of 28 battle honours emblazoned on the drums of the Regimental Band. The drum banners carried by the drum horse display the Royal Coat of Arms as befits the Sovereign's Household Cavalry. The regiment has taken part in all of the major wars in which Britain has been involved, the latest being the Gulf War in 1991, where they fought as part of the Armoured Brigade.

Musician

The 'Albert' pattern helmet, instituted in 1842, is made of white metal with a spike screwed to the top on which the plume is mounted. On the rear is a seam of brass ornamentation, which is normally hidden by the plume. The front plate is richly decorated with brass ornamentation with an eight pointed white metal star in the centre on which is surmounted the regimental badge. On the left is a brass decoration of laurel leaves and on the right the decoration is of oak leaves and acorns. These join in the centre just above the peak, the lower rim of which is edged in brass. On either side of the helmet is a brass rosette of 2¼″ in diameter. These hold the curb chain in position. The curb chain is made up of brass links mounted on black leather backing and it is worn under the lower lip.

Director of Music in Full Review Order   Frank Tyler)

10

Trumpeter in Full Mounted Review Order

The plume is made of horsehair and hangs at the back of the helmet to a length of 24½″. The 'onion' shape at the top is peculiar to the Life Guards only and is obtained by being tied underneath the dome of the spike when not in use. The cost of each plume is approximately £48. The plumes of all musicians are white, whilst those worn by the Trumpeters are scarlet.

The scarlet tunic has a dark blue collar and cuffs. The collar is 1¾″ in height and is edged with gold braid top and bottom. The braid is laced around the inner edges with gold 'tracing braid' in the form of continuous loops, ominously referred to as 'bullet-hole' braiding. The cuffs are embellished in the same manner. The front of the tunic and the bottom edge is piped in gold, with the rear skirts having scarlet slashes piped in gold. The shoulder cords are of gold interwoven cord and all buttons are 'staybright' of regimental pattern. The pouch belts are made of white leather and are 2¾″ in width, with a scarlet 'flash cord' running through the centre held in place by three leather loops. All fittings are brass. The black pouch is 7″ × 3″ in size, with a brass Royal Coat of Arms in the centre mounted on scarlet backing. The white waist belt and sword slings are made of white leather. All fittings are brass with the belt plate bearing the Royal Coat of Arms.

The breeches, as worn when mounted, date from 1812 and are made of white buckskin. These are accompanied by jackboots made of black leather, with the front extension lined with buckskin. The spurs worn with jackboots are the 1955 pattern, made of steel with steel chains and black leather straps.

When dismounted, bandsmen wear dark blue trousers (or overalls). These have two 1½″ scarlet stripes with a scarlet welt between them, down each outer seam. Wellington boots fitted with box spurs are worn with the trousers.

Trumpet Majors and Non-Commissioned Officers

Trumpet Majors usually hold the rank of Warrant Officer Class 1, however neither they nor other Non-Commissioned Officers of the Household Cavalry wear their badges of rank on the Review Order uniform. Instead they wear gold aiguillettes of varying thickness on the left hand side of the tunic, thus:

Trumpet Major
Band Corporal of Horse – 11 ligne plaited gold cord.
Band Corporal – 11 ligne plaited gold cord, less densely plaited.

Uniform detail of the belt buckle.

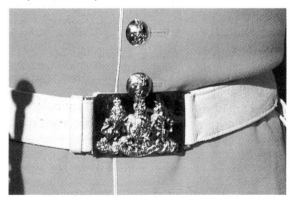

Above: *Detail of Trumpeter's helmet.*
Left and below: *Uniform detail showing the gold braiding on the cuffs and pouch.*

Director of Music

The 'Albert' pattern helmet is made of white metal, the same as for the musicians, with the difference of all the ornamentation being in gilt instead of brass. The lower rim is also edged in gilt and the plume is made of white horsehair.

The scarlet tunic has dark blue velvet collar and cuffs, with dark blue piping down the front and around the bottom edge. The collar is 2¼″ in height and edged with gold oak leaf braiding around the top. Either side, at the front, the collar has the addition of gold laurel leaves with oak leaves and acorns. The cuffs are similarly decorated with the laurel leaves and oak leaves forming a pattern filling the whole of the cuff. The rear skirts are embellished with two rows of three blocks of gold laurel leaf and oak leaf embroidery. All buttons are gilt of regimental pattern. The shoulder cords are of gold interwoven cord with the badges of rank sewn upon them. Badges of rank are embroidered with gold and silver wire. A gold cord aiguillette is worn on the right hand side of the tunic, with one end adjoined to the shoulder cord and the other attached to the top button of the tunic. Officers aguillettes are made of 15 ligne plaited gold wire basket cord.

On State occasions a gold lace pouch belt is worn. It is 2⅜″ in width with dark blue velvet edging and backed with red leather. A crimson 'flash cord' runs through the centre. The black pouch is 8¾″ × 3¾″ in size and bears a gilt regimental cypher with a silver garter star in the centre. All fittings are gilt. The gold lace waist belt is 1¾″ wide and has red leather backing. The belt plate is made of frosted gilt and embellished with the star and collar of the Order of the Garter with a crown above. All other fittings are gilt. Sword slings are the same as the waist belt, being only 1″ wide.

On all other occasions a white pouch belt is worn that is 2½″ in width, with a crimson 'flash cord' through the centre. As with the gold lace pouch belt all fittings are gilt and the same pouch is worn.

Directors of Music carry a State sword of

Bass Drummer and Side Drummer in Full Dismounted Review Order. Frank Tyler

45″ in length, housed in a silver plated scabbard. On State occasions the sword buff is of red leather with a white border. On all other occasions the sword buff is plain white leather. Sword buffs are fitted to the inside of the guard to show through the open pattern. The sword knot is made of white leather with a gold bullion and tassel at the end.

The white breeches are the same as those worn by the musicians and the only difference in the high jackboots is that they are made of a better quality leather.

The dark blue trousers are also the same as those worn by the musicians, with the boots being of better quality.

Drum Horses

By tradition all drum horses are either piebald or skewbald and named after famous military heroes, such as Cicero, Pompey and more recently Leonidus. On average the drum horses are approximately 17 hands in height and take around 1½″ years to train.

The harness and saddlery are all made of black leather with steel and brass fittings. The brow band, nose band and cross piece are all ornately decorated with brass. The reins are crimson leather edged with gold braid and the breastplate has a silver Star and Garter design in the centre. The throat plume for the drum horse of the Life Guards is red and black horsehair. The saddle cover is made of white sheepskin and is worn over the half shabraque. The half shabraque is of a similar pattern to that used by the Director of Music with the only differences being there is no front portion and the basic colour is crimson and not dark blue.

The silver kettledrums are fully covered by

drum banners on regular parades, but have the banners draped half way down on ceremonial occasions. They are carried on the horses withers attached to padded drum pads when on informal parades and on State occasions the drums are carried a little higher.

The drum banners measure 24″ deep × 48″ in width and they are made of crimson damask, edged with gold braid and fringe. The Royal Coat of Arms is embroidered in the centre using gold and silver wire and the appropriately coloured silks. Either side of the Royal Coat of Arms are crowns in full colour, whilst above the central crown are two cherubs with gold wings.

The Trumpet banners measure 16″ deep × 20″ in width, and have the same Royal design as that displayed on the drum banners.

Musical Instruments

The State trumpets carried by the Trumpeters are silver plated, with the banners attached underneath by clip.

Other than the clarinets, which are polished black wood with silver keys, and the piccolo, which is silver plated, all instruments carried by the bandsmen are of a gold lacquer finish.

The Drum Horse in the full splendour of State Dress. Belisarius wearing the livery of the Life Guards at the Royal Tournament.

Above: *Bass Drum.* Left: *Bass Drum.* Frank Tyler

One of a pair of silver kettledrums presented to the Regiment by King William IV in 1831.

Above and below: *The Band of the Life Guards in Full Dismounted Review Order. Note the position of the Director of Music, in the centre of the band formation.* Alan Caton

Above and below: *The band of the Blues & Royals in Full Dismounted Review Order.* Alan Caton

THE BLUES & ROYALS (ROYAL HORSE GUARDS & 1st DRAGOONS)

BATTLE HONOURS

TANGIER 1622-80
DETTINGEN
WARBURG
BEAUMONT
WILLEMS
FUENTES D'ONOR
PENINSULA
WATERLOO
BALAKLAVA
SEVASTOPOL
TEL-EL-KEBIR
EGYPT 1882
RELIEF OF KIMBERLEY
PAARDEBURG
RELIEF OF LADYSMITH
SOUTH AFRICA 1899-1902
LE CATEAU
MARNE 1914
MESSINES 1914
YPRES 1914, 1915, 1917
GHELUVELT
FREZENBERG
LOOS

ARRAS 1917
SOMME 1918
AMIENS
HINDENBURG LINE
CAMBRAI 1918
SAMBRE
PURSUIT TO MONS
FRANCE AND FLANDERS 1914-18
SOULEUVRE
BRUSSELS
NEDERRIJN
RHINE
NORTH-WEST EUROPE 1944-5
IRAQ 1941
PALMYRA
SYRIA 1941
KNIGHTSBRIDGE
EL ALAMEIN
ADVANCE ON TRIPOLI
NORTH AFRICA 1941-3
SICILY 1943
ITALY 1943-4
FALKLAND ISLANDS 1982

Colonel-in-Chief
HM The Queen

Motto
'Honi soit qui mal y pense' (Evil be to him who evil thinks)

History
Formed on the 26 March 1969 by the amalgamation of The Royal Horse Guards (The Blues) and the 1st (Royal) Dragoons.

Home Headquarters
Horse Guards, Whitehall, London SW1A 2YA

Regimental Association
Horse Guards, Whitehall, London SW1 2YA

Regimental Museum
The Household Cavalry Museum, Combermere Barracks, Windsor, Berks.

Marches

Quick march	Grand March from 'Aida' Regimental March of the Royal Dragoons
Slow March	Slow March of the Blues & Royals
Trot Past	Keel Row

Distinctions

The silver kettledrums carried by the drum horses today were presented to the Royal Horse Guards (The Blues) in 1805 by King George III, a year after the regiment moved to London to form part of the Household Brigade. In April 1961 the Lord Mayor and City of London granted the 1st (Royal) Dragoons the distinction of being privileged Regiment of the City. On 8 May 1965 The Royal Horse Guards were granted the 'Freedom of the Royal Borough of Windsor', along with the Life Guards. This means that both regiments may parade through the Royal Borough of Windsor with bayonets fixed and colours unfurled.

There are no less than 46 battle honours emblazoned on the drums of the regimental band. The drum banners carried by the drum

Cuff detail of the Director of Music's Full Review Uniform.

horse display the Royal Coat of Arms, as do those of the Life Guards. So many battle honours to be displayed is very impressive. From one of the earliest battle honours known, Tangiers 1662-80, to the last battle honour to be awarded in the British army, The Falkland Islands 1982, the Blues & Royals have surely earned their place in British history. During the Falklands Campaign the regiment had three members mentioned in dispatches and brought home two Panhard armoured cars as trophies of war!

Opposite page: *Front and rear view of the Director of Music in Full Dismounted Review Order.* Frank Tyler

Below: *Full Mounted Review Order, front and rear view.*

Below right: *Detail of the breeches, jackboots and spurs worn by the Life Guards and the Blues & Royals when Full Review Order is worn.*

Above: *Detail of the front plate of the 'Albert' pattern helmet.*

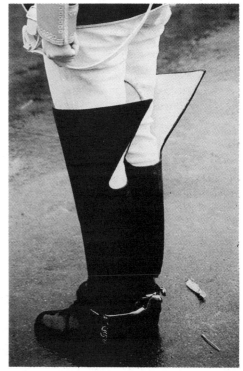

Musician

As for the Life Guards, the 'Albert' pattern helmet is worn, made of white metal with brass fittings and ornamentation. The front plate design has a similar star and plate as for the Life Guards, but the surrounding leaves are all laurel leaves. The curb chain is worn under the chin and the scarlet horsehair plume hangs straight from the top of the spike (unlike the Life Guards, who have an 'onion' shape at the top).

The dark blue tunic has scarlet collars and cuffs. The gold braiding on the collar and cuffs is of the same pattern as that worn by the Life Guards, with the exception that the 'tracing braid' around the inside of the collar ends in a single loop at the front. Gold piping edges the front of the tunic and around the lower edge, but unlike the Life Guards who have buttons on the rear skirt, the musicians of the Blues & Royals do not. The Blues & Royals wear shoulder cords of gold interwoven cord and all buttons are 'stay-bright' of regimental pattern.

The pouch belt, pouch, waist belt and sword slings are the same as those described for the Life Guards.

The breeches, jackboots and spurs, worn for all mounted ceremonial occasions are the same as those worn by the Life Guards. However, the trousers worn for dismounted duties are dark blue with a 2¾″ wide scarlet stripe down each outer seam. The wellington boots and box spurs remain the same.

Trumpet Major and Non-Commissioned Officers

The uniform and method of wearing aiguillettes to identify these ranks are the same as those for the Life Guards. This system is peculiar only to the Household Cavalry.

Director of Music

The Director of Music wears the same 'Albert' pattern helmet as the musicians, with all the ornamentation being gilt instead of brass. The

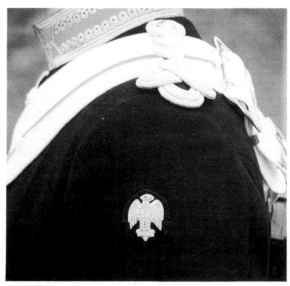

Above: *Detail of the Eagle worn on the left arm by all ranks.*

Left: *Detail of the pouch showing Royal cypher.*

En-route to the Major General's inspection. The Director of Music is followed by the Regiment's two Drum Horses, Belisarius (left) and Caractacus (right). Frank Tyler

scarlet plume is 19″ in length and made of Yak hair at a cost of £105.

The dark blue tunic has scarlet collars and cuffs. All gold piping and laurel leaf decoration on the collar and cuffs is the same as that described for the Life Guards and like the musicians of the Blues & Royals a gilt eagle is worn on the upper part of the left sleeve. Shoulder cords and the aiguillette are as for the Director of Music of the Life Guards.

The pouch belt is made of gold lace of regimental pattern, 2⅜″ in width with a crimson silk centre line over which the crimson 'flash cord' runs. The black pouch is 6½″ × 3¾″ in size and bears a gilt Royal Coat of Arms in the centre. The waist belt, worn with the gold pouch belt on all State duties, is 1¼″ wide and is made of gold regimental lace with a crimson welt running through the centre. All fittings are gilt and the belt plate is frosted gilt with the Royal Coat of Arms in the centre. On all other occasions a white leather pouch belt, as for the Life Guards Officer,

is worn and a white leather waist belt with a gilt plate bearing the St Edward's crown in the centre.

As for the Director of Music of the Life Guards, the director of Music of the Blues & Royals also carries a State sword. The sword buff worn on all occasions is of white leather and the sword knot is made entirely of crimson and gold thread with a gold bullion and tassel. The sword slings for State occasions are of crimson leather edged with gold regimental lace. For other duties the sword slong is made of white leather.

The white breeches, jackboots and spurs are the same as those worn by the musicians of the Blues & Royals, with the boots being of better quality.

The trousers, wellington boots and box spurs are also the same as those worn by the musicians.

Drum Horses

As with the Life Guards, all drum horses are either piebald or skewbald and named after famous military heroes, for example Caractacus, Hector and the present drum horse, Belisarius.

Belisarius (or Basil as he is affectionately

known) is a grey Clydesdale from Fife in Scotland and stands approximately 18 hands in height. He is a firm favourite with the Blues & Royals and one drummer has even said that 'Basil is the best horse I have ever ridden!'

Drum horses eat half a bag of mixed bran and nuts, and half a bale of hay per day in addition to the occasional apple and, as in Basil's case, white mints!

All harnessing and saddlery is as described for the drum horses of the Life Guards, with the exception of the throat plume which is scarlet horsehair, and a black sheepskin saddle cover. The half shabraque is exactly the same as that used by the Director of Music for the Blues & Royals, with the front half cut off.

The silver drums carried by the drum horse have a total weight of 118 lbs of pure silver and each drum has been estimated to a value of over £1m. The inscription on each drum reads:

'Given by King George III April 23rd 1805 To his Royal Regiment of Horse Guards as a testimonial of its honourable and military conduct on all occasions.'

The Drum banners, trumpet banners and musical instruments are the same as those described for the Life Guards.

Below: *One of a pair of silver kettledrums presented to the Royal Horse Guards (Blues) in 1805 by King George III.*

Below left: *Fitting the kettledrums to the Drum Horse, 'Caractacus', at the Royal Windsor Horse Show.* Frank Tyler

Opposite page, bottom right: *'Caractacus' at the Royal Tournament.*

Right: *Musicians in Full Dismounted Review Order.*
Frank Tyler

Below; *'Belisarius' at Knightsbridge Barracks, London.*

Bottom: *Picquet Line at the Putney Show. A welcomed break for both musicians and horses.*

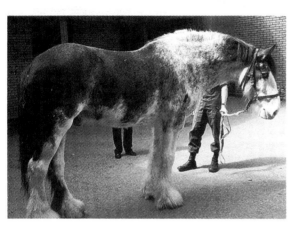

State Dress

For all normal duties the musicians and trumpeters of the Household Cavalry wear the Review Order uniform of their respective regiments, however for all State duties they wear 'State Dress' (otherwise known as 'The Gold Kit').

The term 'State Duties' refers to all occasions where HM The Queen is present, or close members of the Royal Family, and since the turn of the century it is also worn in the presence of the Lord Mayor of London on official occasions at the Guildhall and Mansion House.

State Dress is worn on these occasions by all musicians and trumpeters of the Household Cavalry and by the Drum Majors of the Brigade of Guards. It has changed very little since the time of King Charles II, for at that time it was the Royal Livery.

The tunic is of Tudor design, weighing approximately 25 lbs. It is made of crimson velvet, heavily embroidered and laced with wide gold braid. On the front and rear of the tunic is the Royal Cypher, made from gold and silver

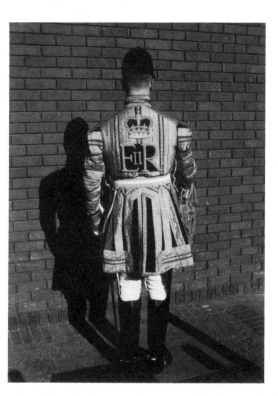

wire. The 'jockey cap' worn with the tunic is made of dark blue velvet.

In the Household Cavalry the tunic is worn with white buckskin breeches and jackboots, whether they are mounted or dismounted.

In the Brigade of Guards, the Drum Majors wear the tunic with white buckskin breeches, white buckskin gaiters (also known as 'spatter-dashes') and black boots. Around the waist they wear a crimson apron that is edged with a gold fringe and fastened at the front with a clasp of the respective regimental cypher. In addition they wear the richly embroidered Regimental Drum Major sash that display their regimental cypher and battle honours. The cost of a complete Drum Major's State Dress is approximately £3500!

Opposite page above: A Drum Horse of the Blues & Royals, 'Caractacus', accompanied by four mounted trumpeters. All musicians are wearing the State Dress. Frank Tyler

Bottom: Rear view of the Kettle Drummer wearing State Dress.

Left and right above: *Rear and front views of the State Dress worn by Household Cavalry trumpeters.*

Below: *The dark blue velvet 'Jockey Cap'.*

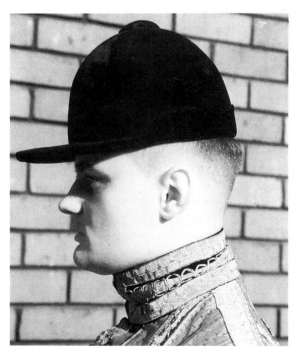

Left: *detail showing crests on front of Tunic.*

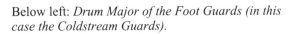

Below left: *Drum Major of the Foot Guards (in this case the Coldstream Guards).*

Below: *Detail of the crimson apron worn by the Drum Major.*

THE BRIGADE OF GUARDS

There are five foot regiments which form the Brigade of Guards:

The Grenadier Guards
The Coldstream Guards
The Scots Guards
The Irish Guards
The Welsh Guards

Each of the regiments has their own Regimental Band with its own Director of Music. In addition each regiment has a Corps of Drums under the direct supervision of the Drum Major and, as in the case of the Scots Guards and the Irish Guards, a Pipe Band under the direct supervision of a Pipe Major.

The differences shown on the uniforms vary according to each regiment and will be dealt with under their respective heading, however the basic design of the ceremonial uniform for the bandsmen is consistent throughout.

The headdress worn by the bandsmen is known as a bearskin. It is made from the fur of the Canadian Black Bear and the curb chain, made of brass links with black leather backing, is worn under the lower lip.

The scarlet serge tunic has a dark blue collar piped white around the top, this piping continuing down the front edge of the tunic. Each regiment has its own badge that is worn on the collar either side at the front (also referred to as 'collar dogs'). The shoulder straps and detachable wings are dark blue edged in ½" gold braid, with an embroidered regimental cypher on each strap.

The cuffs are dark blue edged with white piping and have white cuff slashes grouped according to the regiment. Similarly the white skirt slashes at the rear are grouped according to the regiment, edged with dark blue piping and split into two sides by white piping down the centre.

Rank insignia is worn on the right arm only as follows:

Corporal	Two white chevrons on the upper arm.
Lance Sergeant	Three white chevrons on the upper arm.
Sergeant	Three gold chevrons on the upper arm and a crimson sash is worn over the right shoulder. This rank is sometimes referred to as Gold Sergeant.
Colour Sergeant	Three gold chevrons with the regimental colour superimposed in the centre, worn on the upper arm. A crimson sash is worn over the right shoulder.
Company Sgt/Major	The regimental colour is worn on the upper arm and a crimson sash is worn over the right shoulder
Warrant Officer Class II	A gold crown surrounded by gold laurel leaves is worn on the lower arm, just above the cuff. A crimson sash is worn over the right shoulder.

A Band Sergeant Major can be either a CSM or a WO II depending on the band. These two ranks have the distinction of gold braid halfway round the collar, two bands of gold braid 20mm in width around the cuffs and all slashes being of gold lace, Band Sergeant Majors are the only NCOs to carry a sword when on parade. This is the standard Guards pattern sword with white leather sword slings and white sword knot. It is worn high on the waist belt with the guard to the rear. All other ranks have a bayonet and white leather music pouch fixed to the white leather waist belt at the rear. All buttons are 'staybright' of regimental pattern.

An early history regarding drummers indicate that they held a position of considerable importance. During the reign of Queen Elizabeth I, one historian states that all of Her Majesty's drummers were required to speak a foreign language, as they were often sent to discuss terms with enemy forces and get enemy prisoners to disclose their secrets. As they were in such close connection with the Royal Court they were also required not to disclose any State secrets they had heard!

For a long period the regimental drummers were all boys, often travelling abroad with their regiment to various theatres of war. However, the atrocities committed by the Zulu warriors at Isandhlwana, in which many drummer boys were brutally mutilated beyond recognition, horrified the military authorities (as well as the British public) and after this action drummer boys were only permitted to learn the trade in their home barracks and were never allowed to accompany their regiment into the field of battle again.

The headdress of the Corps of Drums is made in the same way as the bearskin worn by the bandsmen, with the only difference in the shape. The lower edge is trimmed away at the back to a point, giving the bearskin a shorter rounder appearance.

The scarlet tunic has a dark blue collar edged around the top with white lace bearing a blue 'fleur-de-lys' design. The 'fleur-de-lys' was originally part of the Royal Coat of Arms and thus the lace worn by the drummers maintains the present day Royal connection with medieval England. The collar is covered all round by a dark blue and white fringe. The shoulder straps and wings are dark blue, similarly edged with the same lace, with the wings having the dark blue and white fringe along the edges. The same pattern lace continues down the front edge of the tunic and is arranged in rows across the chest according to the button distribution for each regiment. The dark blue cuffs are also edged with the lace, with the white cuff slashes being replaced with it also. The lace is heavily embellished on the sleeves, going the full length front and back and joined on the outer side by more lace in evenly spaced 'inverted chevrons'. This lace also appears on the back of the tunic as well as replacing the piping and slashes on the rear skirt.

Drum Majors have a similar style of scarlet tunic with all the lace being replaced by gold regimental braid, bearing the rank insignia of four inverted chevrons on the lower right sleeve, just above the cuff. In addition the Drum Major wears the respective Drum Major's sash and carries the regimental mace. All Drum Majors carry a sword, slung on white leather sword slings and wear white gloves when on parade.

Trousers for the Regimental Band and the Corps of Drums are the same. Dark blue (almost black) with a single thin scarlet stripe (or 'welt') down each outer seam. The boots that are worn by all, are the standard issue black army parade boots, highly polished.

The Directors of Music wear the same uniform as other serving Officers in the Brigade of Guards.

The black bearskin is taller and more finely tailored, as is the scarlet tunic. The dark blue collar is piped white around the top with gold braid edging the blue, top and bottom. The front of the collar has gold lace going half way round at either side with a silver and gilt regimental badge in the centre. Shoulder straps are dark blue with two rows of gold braid around the edge. Badges of rank are worn towards the outer edge. White piping edges the front of the tunic. The rear skirt has gold braid outlining the gold lace slashes, with white piping edging it and separating the two halves. Two rows of gold braid edge the dark blue cuffs, with the slashes being of gold regimental lace.

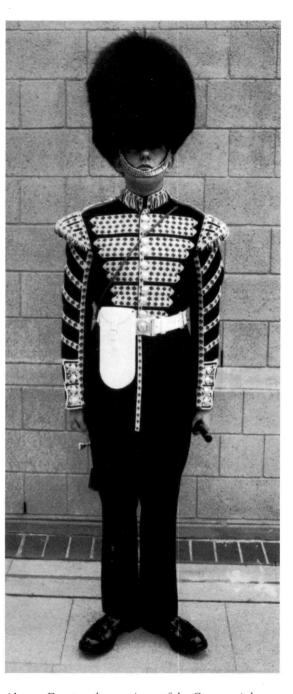

Above: *Front and rear views of the Ceremonial Uniform worn by musicians of the Corps of Drums.*

At all times the Director of Music carries a sword when on parade, the sword sling being white leather for normal duties and gold with red leather backing for State ceremonial occasions. A crimson sash is worn around the waist, but this is changed for a crimson and gold sash for State duties. White gloves are worn at all times.

Trousers are dark blue (almost black) with a wide scarlet stripe down each outer seam.

THE GRENADIER GUARDS

Colonel-in-Chief
HM The Queen

Motto
'Honi soit qui mal y pense' (Evil be to him who evil thinks)

History
The Grenadier Guards were originally raised in 1656 as Wentworth's Foot Guards, whilst in exile with King Charles II. The regiment was amalgamated with Russell's Foot Guards in 1665 to form the 1st Regiment of Foot Guards. Re-designated the 1st or Grenadier Regiment of Foot Guards in 1815.

Home Headquarters
Wellington Barracks, Birdcage Walk, London SW1E 6HQ

Regimental Association
Wellington Barracks, Birdcage Walk, London SW1E 6HQ

Regimental Museum
The Guards Museum, Wellington Barracks, Birdcage Walk, London SW1E 6HQ

Marches
Quick march	The British Grenadiers
	The Grenadiers March
Slow march	Scipio
	The Duke of York

BATTLE HONOURS

TANGIER 1680	MARNE 1914
NAMUR 1695	AISNE 1914
GIBRALTAR 1704-5	YPRES 1914, 1917
	LOOS
BLENHEIM	SOMME 1916, 1918
RAMILLIES	CAMBRAI 1917, 1918
OUDENARDE	ARRAS 1918
MALPLAQUET	HAZEBROUCK
DETTINGEN	HINDENBURG LINE
LINCELLES	FRANCE AND
EGMONT OP ZEE	FLANDERS 1914-18
	DUNKIRK 1940
CORUNNA	MONT PINÇON
BARROSA	NIJMEGEN
NIVE	RHINE
PENINSULA	MARETH
WATERLOO	MEDJEZ PLAIN
ALMA	SALERNO
INKERMAN	MONTE CAMINO
SEVASTOPOL	ANZIO
TEL-EL-KEBIR	GOTHIC LINE
EGYPT	
SUAKIN 1885	
KHARTOUM	
MODDER RIVER	
SOUTH AFRICA 1899-1902	

Bearskin of the Grenadier Guards.

Detail of the shoulder strap.

Distinctions

The first mention of a Regimental Band is in the Royal Warrant of 1685, whereby King Charles II authorised the engagement of 12 Hautboys. This small group was gradually increased to 15 Hautboys in 1699, added to by the addition of 2 French Horns in 1725 and some bugle horns in 1772. By 1794 the Band had a strength of 16 musicians and 'Turkish Music' (Negro Time-Beaters who played the bass drum, cymbals and tambourine). Today there are approximately 48 musicians in the Regimental Band and the Bass drummers have retained the title of 'Time Beater'.

The Grenadier Guards have been granted the 'Freedom of the City of London', this honour having been gained by the 3rd Battalion in 1915.

There are a total of 44 battle honours emblazoned on the drums of the Regimental Band, bearing testimony to the heroic deeds of the Regiment for over 300 years. Thirteen Victoria Crosses have been awarded to soldiers of the Grenadier Guards: four in the Crimean War, seven in the First World War and two in the Second World War.

Uniform Distinctions

A white horsehair plume is worn by all ranks on the left hand side of the bearskin.

The regimental badge of a 'grenade fired

proper' is worn on the collar, either side at the front. This distinction was granted after the victory at The Battle of Waterloo in 1815. The shoulder straps bear the badge of the Royal Cypher, the blue Garter with 'ER' in the centre and surmounted by a crown.

All buttons, cuff slashes, skirt slashes and lace on the chest (for the Corps of Drums) are singularly spaced.

Drum straps are dark blue leather edged either side with gold braid. Bass drummers of the Regimental Band wear a scarlet apron, whilst

Left: *Side Drummer in full Ceremonial Uniform, Regimental Band.*

Right: *Bass Drum.*

the bass drummer of the Corps of Drums wears a white leather apron. The cymbalist of the Regimental Band also wears a scarlet apron to protect his uniform from the polished cymbals. All brass instruments have a gold lacquer finish.

34

Below: *Shoulder strap showing gold braiding and embroidered garter, Band Sergeant Major, Grenadier Guards.*

Details of Cuff Slashes:
Top left: *Director of Music.*
Above: *Band Sergeant Major.* Below: *Other ranks.*

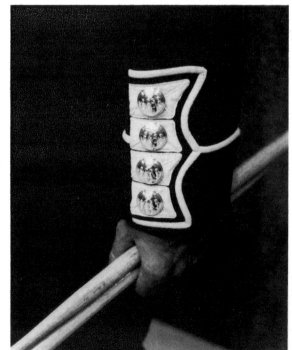

Above: *The Corps of Drums on parade, Grenadier Guards.* Frank Tyler

Right: *Badge of Rank of the Company Sergeant Major, Grenadier Guards.* Frank Tyler.

Below: *Trumpet Banner, Grenadier Guards*

THE COLDSTREAM GUARDS

BATTLE HONOURS

TANGIER 1680	MARNE 1914
NAMUR 1695	AISNE 1914
GIBRALTAR 1704-5	YPRES 1914, 1917
	LOOS
OUDENARDE	SOMME 1916, 1918
MALPLAQUET	CAMBRAI 1917, 1918
DETTINGEN	ARRAS 1918
LINCELLES	HAZEBROUCK
TALAVERA	HINDENBURG LINE
BARROSA	DUNKIRK 1940
FUENTES D'ONOR	MONT PINÇON
	RHINELAND
SALAMANCA	NORTH-WEST
NIVE	EUROPE 1940,
PENINSULA	1944-5
WATERLOO	SIDI BARRANI
ALMA	TUNIS
INKERMAN	SALERNO
SEVASTOPOL	MONTE ORNITO
TEL-EL-KEBIR	ITALY 1943-5
EGYPT 1882	
SUAKIN 1885	
MODDER RIVER	
SOUTH AFRICA 1899-1902	
RETREAT FROM MONS	

Colonel-in-Chief
HM The Queen

Motto
'Nulli Secundus' (Second to none)

History
The Coldstream Guards were raised in August 1650 as Monk's Regiment of Foot, placed in the King's service in 1661 as The Lord General's Regiment of Foot Guards and re-designated the 2nd or Coldstream Guards in 1670.

Home Headquarters
Wellington Barracks, Birdcage Walk, London SW1E 6HQ

Regimental Association
Wellington Barracks, Birdcage Walk, London SW1E 6HQ

Regimental Museum
The Guards Museum, Wellington Barracks, Birdcage Walk, London SW1E 6HQ

Marches
Quick march   Milanollo
Slow march   Figaro

Full ceremonial uniform of the Director of Music.

Distinctions

The motto 'Second to none' signifies the fact that the Regiment is actually the oldest of all the Foot Guards and it does not accept the position of being designated the 2nd Regiment, having entered the King's service after the Grenadier Guards.

The Regimental Band officially became recognized on 16 May 1785 with a total strength of 12 musicians.

The Coldstream Guards have been granted the 'Freedom of the City of London'.

A total of 42 battle honours are borne on the

drums of the Regimental Band, thus bearing testimony to the many theatres of war in which the Coldstream Guards have participated. The regiment has also had its share of heroes with no less than thirteen members having been awarded the Victoria Cross: four in the Crimean War, seven in the First World War and two in the Second World War.

Uniform Distinctions

For all musicians a 6½" scarlet horsehair plume is worn on the right hand side of the bearskin. Staff Sergeants and Warrant Officers wear a 7" scarlet feather plume and the Director of Music wears a 9" scarlet feather plume on the right hand side of the bearskin.

The regimental badge of a Garter star is worn on the collar, at either side at the front. The shoulder straps bear the Tudor Rose.

All buttons, cuff slashes, skirt slashes and lace across the chest (for the Corps of Drums) are grouped in pairs.

The equipment and instruments of the Band and Corps of Drums are as described for the Grenadier Guards.

Left: Officer's bearskin. Note the height of the bearskin and the detail of the collar on the tunic.

Above:
Warrant Officer's bearskin. Note the shape of the bearskin and the detail of the collar on the tunic.

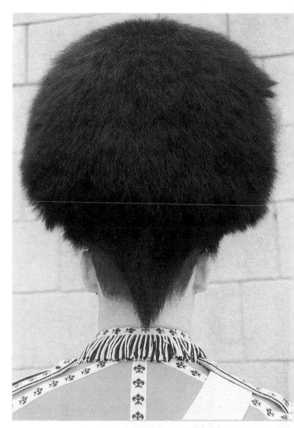

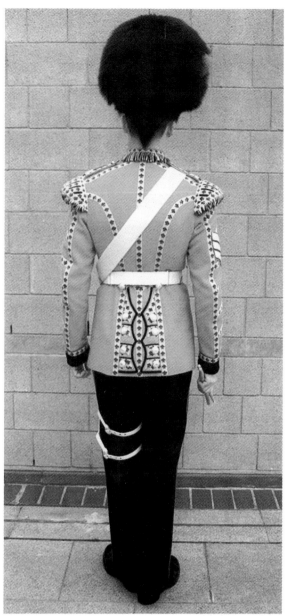

Opposite page:

Top left: *Bearskin of the Corps of Drums. Note the shape at the bottom.*

Top right: *Bearskin of the Corps of Drums showing the 'cut away' shape at the rear.*

Below left: *Bass Drum of the Regimental Band.*

Below right: *Other ranks' bearskin.*

Side Drummer, Corps of Drums, front and rear views.

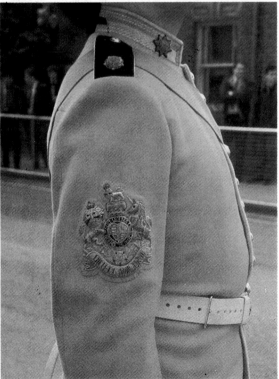

Badges of Rank:

Top left: *Company Sergeant Major.* Frank Tyler

Top right: *Lance Sergeant. Note the lace detail on the arm and cuff of the Corps of Drums.*

Left: *Regimental Sergeant Major.* Frank Tyler

Opposite page: *Drum Major in ceremonial uniform.*

THE SCOTS GUARDS

Colonel-in-Chief
HM The Queen

Motto
'Nemo me impune lacessit' (Let no one provoke me with impunity)

History
The Scots Guards were raised in March 1642 as Argyll's Regiment and disbanded in 1651 after the Battle of Worcester. Re-formed in 1660 as the Scotch Guards, then designated the 3rd Regiment of Foot Guards in 1712 and the Scots Fusilier Guards in 1831. Finally being given the title of the Scots Guards in 1877.

Home Headquarters
Wellington Barracks, Birdcage Walk, London SW1E 6HQ

Regimental Association
Wellington Barracks, Birdcage Walk, London SW1E 6HQ

Regimental Museum
The Guards Museum, Wellington Barracks, Birdcage Walk, London SW1E 6HQ

Marches
Quick march   Hi'lan Laddie
Slow march   Garb of Old Gaul

BATTLE HONOURS

NAMUR 1695
DETTINGEN
LINCELLES
TALAVERA
BARROSA
FUENTES D'ONOR
SALAMANCA
NIVE
PENINSULA
WATERLOO
ALMA
INKERMAN
SEVASTOPOL
TEL-EL-KEBIR
EGYPT 1882
SUAKIN 1885
MODDER RIVER
SOUTH AFRICA 1899-1902
RETREAT FROM MONS
MARNE 1914
AISNE 1914
YPRES 1914, 1917
FESTUBERT 1915
LOOS

SOMME 1916, 1918
CAMBRAI 1917, 1918
HINDENBURG LINE
FRANCE AND FLANDERS 1914-18
QUARRY HILL
RHINELAND
NORTH-WEST EUROPE 1944-5
GAZALA
MEDENINE
DJEBEL BOU AOUKAZ 1943
NORTH AFRICA 1941-3
MONTE CAMINO
ANZIO
ITALY 1943-5
FALKLAND ISLANDS 1982

Distinctions

Although Commanding Officers were allowed to have their own piper (unpaid!) from the formation of the Regiment, it was not until 1856 that one Pipe Major and five Pipers were officially authorised (with pay!). In 1946 the Scots Guards received the honour of the 'Freedom of the City of Brussels', after taking part in a parade at the Palace of Justice.

The drums of the Regimental Band are emblazoned with 39 Battle honours from Namur of 1695 to the Falkland Islands of 1982. Their latest encounter with enemy forces, however, came in 1991 when the Regiment was deployed in the Gulf War.

Eleven members of the Scots Guards have been awarded the Victoria Cross: five were won in the Crimean war, five in the First World War and one during the Second World War.

Uniform Distinctions

No plume is worn on the bearskin. This distinction dates back to 1831 when the Regiment adopted the bearskin and assumed its traditional position of always standing in the centre of the line. Thus no distinguishing plume was necessary.

The Thistle of Scotland is worn on the collar, on either side at the front. This dates from 1895 as prior to this date a star was worn. The shoulder straps bear the star of the Order of the Thistle, with a small regimental button through the centre. This is a peculiarity of the Scots Guards.

All buttons, cuff slashes, skirt slashes and lace (for the Corps of Drums) are grouped in three's.

Pipers

Pipers of the Scots Guards wear the traditional black Highland feather bonnet (granted in 1920 by King George V), with red, white and blue dicing around the headband. A large blue over red hackle is worn on the left hand side of the bonnet, held in place by a silver badge. The chin strap is black patent leather.

The doublet is dark blue with white piping and silver buttons. The waist belt and shoulder

Side Drummers, Corps of Drums, in full ceremonial uniform. Frank Tyler

belt (a relic of past days when it was used to carry a sword into battle) is made of black leather with silver plated buckles. All pipers carry a dirk and a sgiandhu, the latter being worn in the top of the right hose. The kilt and plaid is the Royal Stuart tartan, with a large silver regimental brooch holding the plaid in place. The sporran is of white horsehair with three black horsehair plumes hanging from silver holders on the front. This is topped by a silver crest held to the waist belt by silver chains.

The hose has dark red and scarlet crossed diamonds at the top, with scarlet flashes. White spats with silver buttons are worn over their shoes.

The pipes are the traditional three drone set, with a Royal blue bag and Royal Stuart tartan ribbons. The cords and tassels are made up of all the colours found in the Royal Stuart tartan.

Pipe Major

The uniform of the Pipe Major follows that of the piper with the following differences.

All lace and piping is silver, with the rank insignia worn on the lower right sleeve just above the cuff: four silver inverted chevrons with a crown above. The Pipe Major wears a crimson sash, although this is almost concealed by the plaid, and a Scottish broadsword on a black leather Warrant Officer's belt is carried on all occasions.

On State occasions the Pipe Major carries the scarlet and gold regimental pipe banner.

The Pipe Major of the Scots Guards holds the distinction of being the Household Piper to HM The Queen. It is his duty to play before the Royal Household on all State occasions and for these indoor functions he does not wear spats and his boots are traded in for black brogues with silver buckles.

Top: *Bass Drum, Corps of Drums.* Frank Tyler

Right: *Piccolo musician of the Regimental Band. Note the music holder on his wrist!* Frank Tyler

Opposite page: *Drummer and piper of the Pipes and Drums.* Frank Tyler

46

THE IRISH GUARDS

Colonel-in-Chief
HM The Queen

Motto
'Quis separabit' (Who shall separate)

History
The Irish Guards were raised in 1900 by the order of HM Queen Victoria, who wished to commemmorate the bravery displayed by Irish soldiers during the Boer War in South Africa.

Home Headquarters
Wellington Barracks, Birdcage Walk, London SW1E 6HQ

Regimental Association
Wellington Barracks, Birdcage Walk, London SW1E 6HQ

Regimental Museum
The Guards Museum, Wellington Barracks, Birdcage Walk, London SW1E 6HQ

Marches
Quick march   St Patrick's Day
Slow march   Let Erin Remember

Mascot
The Irish Guards are the only regiment within the Brigade of Guards today to have an official mascot. By tradition it is an Irish Wolfhound.

BATTLE HONOURS

RETREAT FROM MONS	NORWAY 1940
MARNE 1914	BOULOGNE 1940
AISNE 1914	MONT PINÇON
YPRES 1914, 1917	NEERPELT
FESTUBERT 1915	NIJMEGEN
LOOS	RHINELAND
SOMME 1916, 1918	NORTH-WEST EUROPE 1944-5
CAMBRAI 1917, 1918	DJEBEL BOU AOUKAZ 1943
HAZEBROUCK	NORTH AFRICA 1943
HINDENBURG LINE	ANZIO

IRISH GUARDS continues on page 57, after the colour section.

GUARDS
IN COLOUR

Right: *Major Roger Tomlinson (Blues & Royals), Senior Director of Music, Household Cavalry, in full Review Order.*

Below: *Rear view of full dress tunic.*

The Drum Horse of the Life Guards, 'Leonidas'. Frank Tyler

Officers shabraque, the Life Guards.

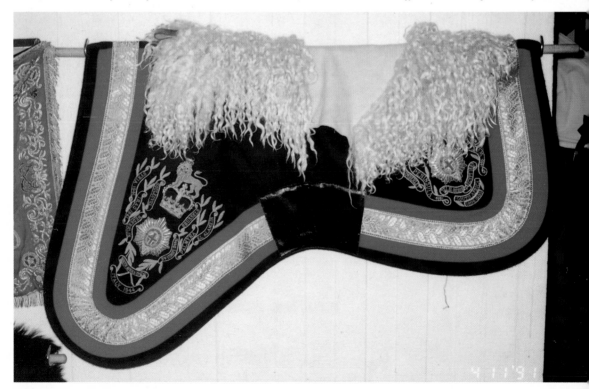

Blues and Royals Drum Horse, 'Belisarius'.
The Blues and Royals.

Below: *Officers shabraque, the Blues and Royals.*

Household Cavalry silver trumpet and banner.

Below: *Drum banner carried by the Household Cavalry.*

Above: Side Drum, the Life Guards.

Right: Major Lane, Director of Music, Life Guards, in full dress.

Below: Side Drum, the Blues and Royals.

Opposite page.

Far left: *Pipe Major, Scots Guards.*

Left: *Side Drummer, the Corps of Drums, Scots Guards.* Frank Tyler

Above left: *Side Drum, The Grenadier Guards.*

Above: *Side Drum, The Coldstream Guards.*

Below left: *Side Drum, The Irish Guards.*

Below: *Side Drum and Cymbals of the Welsh Guards.* Frank Tyler

Above: *Conner and his handler, Irish Guards. Conner is the only official mascot of the Brigade of Guards.*

Left: *Side Drummer, Regimental Band, Irish Guards.*

Below: *Detail of Conner's shabraque showing the Regimental Crest.*

Distinctions

The Regimental Band was formed almost at the same time as the regiment itself and comprised of approximately 35 musicians.

The Pipe Band was not formed until 1916, when they chose to wear the saffron kilt and carry the Irish War Pipe (with two drones). In 1960 they changed to the Scottish Bagpipe with the extra drone.

It is interesting to note that during the Middle Ages both the Irish and the Scots carried bagpipes into battle, which was considered to be a provocative action. King Edward III actually banned the instrument and Oliver Cromwell disliked the bagpipes so much that he threatened to ban anyone who played them to a permanent residency in Barbados!

The drums of the Regimental Band carry 20 battle honours, no mean feat for a comparatively young regiment whose first major action was the First World War. Six Victoria Crosses have been awarded to members of the Regiment: four in the First World War and two in the Second World War.

Previous page: *Director of Music in full ceremonial uniform, front and rear views.*

Opposite page: *Director of Music. Detail of rear skirt slashes (upper left), cuff (upper right) and bearskin (below).*

Authors note:

These are possibly the last photographs taken of Lt. Col. M. Lane, Irish Guards, before his untimely death. A gentleman and fine musician, he is sadly missed by us all.

Below: *Detail of collar and shoulder strap, Director of Music.*

Uniform Distinctions

All musicians wear a 6½″ blue horsehair plume on the right hand side of the bearskin. Staff Sergeants and Warrant Officers wear a 7″ blue feather plume and the Director of Music wears a 9″ feather plume on the right hand side of the bearskin.

As a distinguishing mark of an Irish regiment a shamrock is worn on the collar, on either side at the front. The shoulder straps bear the Star of the Order of St Patrick.

All buttons, cuff slashes, skirt slashes and lace on the chest (for the Corps of Drums) are arranged in groups of four.

Pipers

Pipers of the Irish Guards wear a dark green 'caubeen'. The blue hackle of St Patrick is worn at the front, held in place by a silver regimental badge.

The doublet is dark green with black mohair piping and button loops. All buttons and buckles are silver, with the badges on the collar and shoulder straps being the same as for the bands.

men. The waist belt and cross belt is made of black leather, with white metal fittings and when on parade a knee-length dark green cloak is worn, held in place by a white metal chain. The kilt is the distinctive saffron colour.

The hose is dark green with saffron 'flashes' and the brogues are black.

The bag and ribbons of the bagpipes are all dark green.

Pipe Major

The only differences to distinguish the Pipe Major from the other pipers of the Irish Guards are the following.

A crimson sash is worn across the left shoulder and all piping on the dark green doublet is silver. On the lower right arm, just above the cuff are four inverted silver chevrons with a crown above.

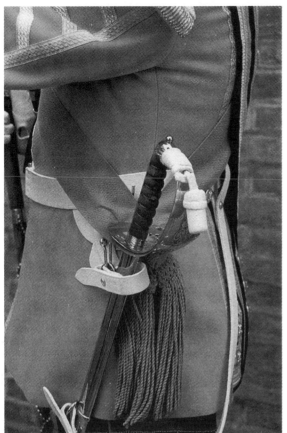

Mascot

An Irish Wolfhound is the traditional mascot of the Irish Guards. The first, Brian Boru, was presented to the Regiment in 1902 and served as the mascot until 1910. The present mascot, Connor, is the 9th Irish Wolfhound to march with the Band and was presented to the Regiment when only three months old by HM The Queen Mother.

When on parade Connor wears a scarlet shabraque with a silver and gilt regimental crest in each rear corner. It is fastened at the neck by three gilt regimental buttons and across the neck by a silver chain mounted on a silver regimental star each side. The thick leather collar has a silver regimental star either side with a brass nameplate on the top.

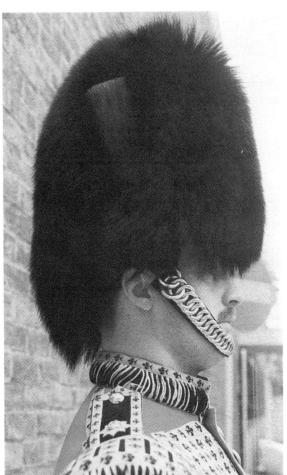

Above left: *Warrant Officer's bearskin.*

Above right: *Other rank's bearskin, Corps of Drums.*

Right: *Detail of the rear skirt slashes of the tunic of the Regimental Band.*

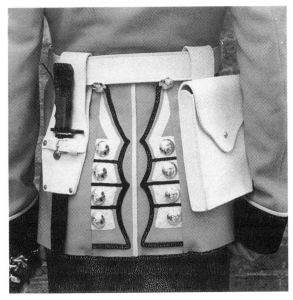

Opposite page:

Top left: *Detail of sword and sword slings worn by the Drum Major.*

Top right: *Detail of the Drum Major's slash.*

Left: *Badge of the Rank of the Company Sergeant Major.*

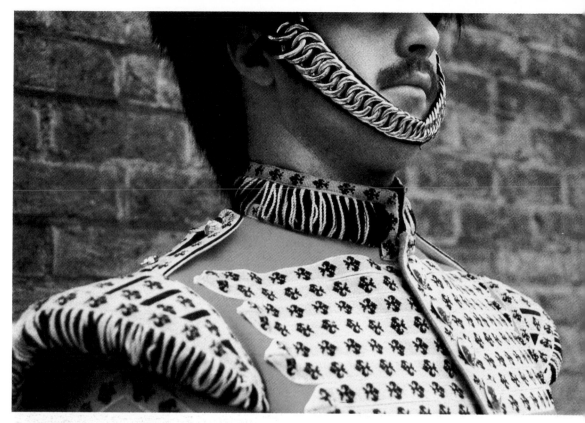

Top: *Detail of the tunic for the Corps of Drums.*

'Conner', the mascot of the Irish Guards. Note the fastening on the shabraque and collar detail.

Top left: *Bass Drum of the Regimental Band.*

Above: *Side Drummer in ceremonial uniform, Regimental Band.*

Left: *Detail of the head of the mace, Pipes & Drums. Irish Guards.*

Piper, Irish Guards, at Chelsea Barracks, London. Jerome Gatehouse

THE WELSH GUARDS

Colonel-in-Chief
HM The Queen

Motto
'Cymru am byth' (Wales for ever)

History
The Welsh Guards were raised on 23 February 1915, by a special order issued by The War Office upon a request from King George V: 'His Majesty The King has been graciously pleased to approve the formation of a Welsh Regiment of Foot Guards to be designated Welsh Guards.'

Home Headquarters
Wellington Barracks, Birdcage Walk, London SW1E 6HQ

Regimental Association
Wellington Barracks, Birdcage Walk, London SW1E 6HQ

Regimental Museum
The Guards Museum, Wellington Barracks, Birdcage Walk, London SW1E 6HQ

Marches
Quick march   Rising of the Lark
Slow march   Men of Harlech

BATTLE HONOURS

LOOS	BOULOGNE 1940
GINCHY	MONT PINÇON
FLERS-COURCELETTE	BRUSSELS
	HECHTEL
MORVAL	FONDOUK
PILCKEM	HAMMAM LIF
POELCAPELLE	MONTE ORNITO
CAMBRAI 1917, 1918	MONTE PICCOLO
BAUME 1918	BATTAGLIA
CANAL DU NORD	FALKLAND ISLANDS 1982
SAMBRE	
DEFENCE OF ARRAS	

Top left Badges of Rank:
Left: *Corporal and* (right:) *Colour Sergeant.*
Frank Tyler

Above: *Drum Major in State Dress.* Frank Tyler

Left: *Badge of Rank of the Company Sergeant Major.* Frank Tyler

The moment every musician dreads, inspection. Here the Director of Music and his band Sergeant Major *checks every minute detail of the Regimental Band, turned out in greatcoat order.* Frank Tyler

The Corps of Drums on parade. Frank Tyler

Distinctions

The Welsh Guards are the youngest regiment in the Brigade of Guards. The Regimental Band was formed on 9 October 1915 with a total of 44 musicians.

There are 21 battle honours emblazoned on the drums of the Regimental Band. Having fought in their first engagement at Loos on 27 September 1915, the Regiment last saw action in the Falkland Islands in 1982 where heavy losses were incurred during their disembarkation at Bluff Cove. Since the formation of the regiment, two Victoria Crosses have been awarded, one in the First World War and one during the Second World War.

Uniform Distinctions

All musicians and Warrant Officers wear a 6″ white-green-white horsehair plume on the left hand side of the bearskin. The Director of Music has a 9″ white-green-white plume made of feathers, worn on the left hand side of the bearskin.

A Welsh leek is worn on both the collar and shoulder straps. The leek has been used as a Welsh emblem from as far back as the seventh century and is still used as such today. Tradition has it that the leek is connected with St David, the Patron Saint of Wales.

All buttons, cuff slashes, skirt slashes and lace on the chest (for the Corps of Drums) are arranged in groups of five.

FORTHCOMING AMALGAMATIONS

THE GUARDS MUSEUM APPEAL

On 4 July 1991 Tom King, the Defence Secretary, announced a dramatic change in the structure of the British Armed Forces. The changes primarily marked the amalgamation of many regiments, thus cutting the number of personnel. The Household Cavalry and the Brigade of Guards will be affected by the following amalgamations or structural changes over the next two years.

The HOUSEHOLD CAVALRY comprising of THE LIFE GUARDS and THE BLUES & ROYALS (ROYAL HORSE GUARDS & 1st DRAGOONS) will combine to form an Armoured Reconnaissance Regiment and The Household Cavalry Mounted Regiment, although both existing regiments will retain their individual identities. The Armoured Reconnaissance Regiment will serve in theatres of conflict, whereas the Household Cavalry Mounted Regiment will be strictly confined to ceremonial duties.

Three Battalions in the Brigade of Guards will be affected by being put into 'suspended animation':
THE 2nd BATTALION GRENADIER
    GUARDS
THE 2nd BATTALION COLDSTREAM
    GUARDS
THE 2nd BATTALION SCOTS GUARDS

An appeal has been launched to provide funds for the maintenance of the Guards Museum and for the acquisition of new items to be displayed in order that the museum will continue into the future. The costs involved in the upkeep of museums is extremely high and any donation large or small, would be of great help. Any contributions, particularly by Deed of Covenant would be greatly appreciated and should be sent to:

The Guards Museum Appeal Office
Wellington Barracks
Birdcage Walk
London SW1E 6HQ

Museums are the heritage of the Nation and the only institutions where past relics and glories can be appreciated. What is happening today will be history tomorrow, so remember the motto 'PROTECT AND PRESERVE' and help if you can.

Above: Director of Music, Blues & Royals. Frank Tyler   Below: *Mounted Officer, Scots Guards.* Frank Tyler

Pride of England. The smartness of the British Guardsman is second to none.